THIS IS HISTORY!

Write Your Own Roman Story

BETH BROOKE

DAVE MARTIN

IAN DAWSON

JOHN MURRAY

The Schools History Project

The Project was set up in 1972, with the aim of improving the study of History for students aged 13–16. This involved a reconsideration of the ways in which History contributes to the educational needs of young people. The Project devised new objectives, new criteria for planning and developing courses, and the materials to support them. New examinations, requiring new methods of assessment, also had to be developed. These have continued to be popular. The advent of GCSE in 1987 led to the expansion of Project approaches into other syllabuses.

The Schools History Project has been based at Trinity and All Saints College, Leeds, since 1978, from where it supports teachers through a biennial Bulletin, regular INSET, an annual Conference and a website (www.tasc.ac.uk/shp).

Since the National Curriculum was drawn up in 1991, the Project has continued to expand its publications, bringing its ideas to courses for Key Stage 3 as well as a range of GCSE and A level specifications.

Words printed in SMALL CAPITALS are defined in the Glossary on pages 56–58.

Latin words appear in a *Latin italic* font and translations are given in the Glossary on pages 56–58.

© Beth Brooke, Dave Martin, Ian Dawson 2001

First published in 2001
by John Murray (Publishers) Ltd
50 Albemarle Street
London W1S 4BD

Layouts by Ken Vail Graphic Design, Cambridge
Artwork by Richard Duszczak, Pete Lawrence, Tony Randell and Steve Smith
Printed and bound by G. Canale, Torino, Italy

A catalogue entry for this book is available from the British Library

ISBN 0 7195 7717 9
Teachers' Resource Book ISBN 0 7195 7718 7

◆ Contents

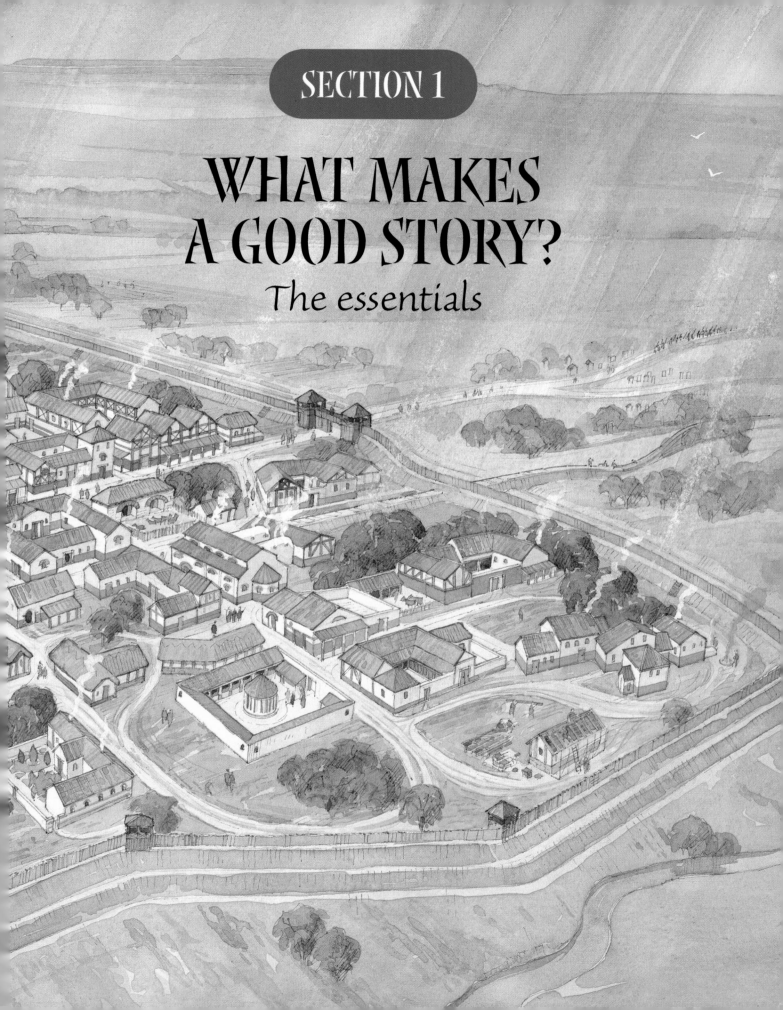

SECTION 1

WHAT MAKES A GOOD STORY?

The essentials

Salvete! WELCOME!
Meet the people who will help you write your Roman story

VESPASIAN

"*SALVETE!*

From Imperator Titus Vespasianus Caesar, Emperor of the Roman world, greetings!

You are here as assistants to the imperial SCRIBE – a beetle of a man, always scuttling around, getting under my feet with his, 'Caesar, when shall we begin the history of your glorious reign?' and his, 'Lordship, the Senate beg you to record the many achievements of your reign!' No matter, you'll find out about him soon enough.

Now, listen: if a record of my reign is truly required, then the people shall have one – and more besides. They shall have a story of themselves and their own times in this, the ninth year of my reign. I have plenty of perfectly good historians, but their writing is dull. What I want is to capture the voices of my people and that's the job I want you to do. You must write stories about the adventures of the ordinary people of my empire.

Old beetle-features will oversee your work, but you will have to start at once. There he is, over there. Make sure you listen carefully …

VALETE!"

"*SALVE*, welcome stranger. I am the Imperial scribe, Canidius.

It is the ninth year of our emperor's glorious reign. Fortunately for us all, he came to power after the civil wars of the Year of the Four Emperors. Yes, four emperors in one year! AD69, the year after the Emperor Nero committed suicide before his enemies could kill him. What a year that was! First there was the Emperor Galba, who was murdered by the Praetorian Guard. Then the Emperor Otho, who committed suicide when his army was defeated. Then the Emperor Vitellius, who was murdered after his army was defeated. And finally, the great Emperor Vespasian, my beloved master.

That was a bad time – Roman soldier fighting Roman soldier, towns destroyed, men, women and children slaughtered. Not even the city of Rome itself escaped the fighting. There was chaos throughout the Empire as towns and people settled old scores.

Anyway, that's not important now. The great Vespasian has changed all that. Now we have a strong emperor with two good sons, Titus and Domitian, to follow him. The Empire is at peace, as you will see for yourself when you visit four of our towns to research your story.

On page 6, I will give you some guidelines for your story, but first meet some of the people and places you might write about. First let me introduce you to the farmer, Petronius, who will show you around his town."

CANIDIUS

Durnovaria

Salve! I am Petronius and this is my town, Durnovaria. I settled here to farm when I left the army. I actually served under Vespasian when he commanded a legion here in Britain.

Durnovaria is a very new town, but we already have an AMPHITHEATRE. The AQUEDUCT to bring in clean drinking water will soon be finished, I hope. Britain is becoming a very civilised province of the Empire. After all, it is nearly twenty years since the terror of Boudicca's revolt. I hope you manage to see our *amphitheatre* and I'd be delighted to show you round the new MOSAIC workshop that I am a partner in.

Lectis Magna

Salve! I am Silvia and this is my city, Lectis Magna. As you can see, this is a fine and ancient city and my family have been important here for generations. I, of course, hold the important post of priestess of Juno, goddess of women and marriage. I hope I have the chance to show you her beautiful temple and perhaps we could pay a visit to the baths. They are rather fine.

Life has been good under Vespasian. The wicked people of the city of Oea and their desert allies, the Garamantes, attacked us in the Year of the Four Emperors, but they have been kept under control by our great Emperor ever since.

Now our city is growing wealthy from the olive oil industry here in Africa. We supply much of the Empire, you know.

◆ Pompeii

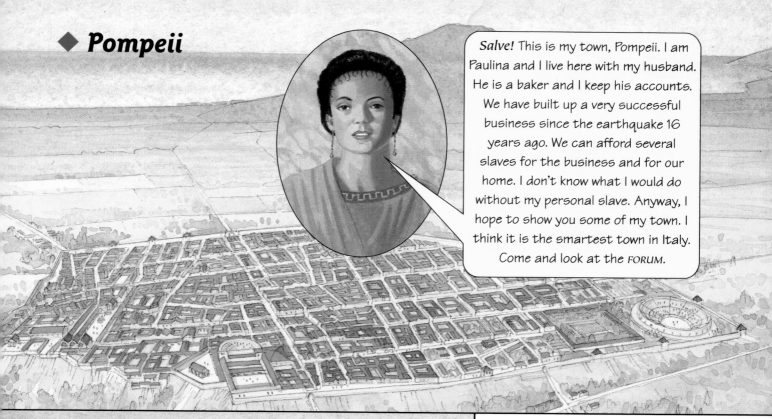

Salve! This is my town, Pompeii. I am Paulina and I live here with my husband. He is a baker and I keep his accounts. We have built up a very successful business since the earthquake 16 years ago. We can afford several slaves for the business and for our home. I don't know what I would do without my personal slave. Anyway, I hope to show you some of my town. I think it is the smartest town in Italy. Come and look at the FORUM.

◆ Curium

Salve! I am Lytras and this is the city of Curium, where my master lives. It is a very ancient city which became Roman when Cyprus became part of the Roman Empire. My master brought me here two years ago after he bought me in the slave market. I am in training as a gladiator. I have already killed five men.

You can choose any of these four towns as the setting for your story.

WHAT CAN YOU SEE, HEAR AND SMELL?

Canidius, the scribe, shows you how to use setting to bring your story to life

"Before you begin you need to know what you have to do. If you are to accomplish the task given to you by the great Vespasian, you must follow the guidance and practice I, Canidius, Imperial Scribe, give you. At the end you will be ready to write your own story. Your work is for the Imperial Library and I have high standards that you must meet. Read this wax tablet carefully, it contains all the instructions you need."

You are going to write a piece of historical fiction set in the year AD 78, during the reign of the Emperor Vespasian. There are a few rules that you have to follow:

* Your story can have up to three characters.
* The action must take place over no more than three days.
* The story must clearly be set in one of the four Roman towns on pages 4–5.

When you plan your story, you must consider:

* the setting
* the characters
* the problem that starts the story off
* the things that happen as a result of the problem – these are called conflicts
* the resolution of the story – how things are worked out in the end.

Remember to use the historical sources in this book to give you ideas about the setting.

Remember to practise the writing techniques you learn from this book.

Remember that a good historical story is one that is interesting and feels authentic.

Before you can write your story, you have to think carefully about its setting. The setting of a story is what provides the background for the action. In a piece of historical fiction, the setting is extra important because it gives the reader details about the period in which the story is set. However, you need to get the balance right – if you give too much detail your story will read like a thinly disguised excuse to teach people about the Romans. Too little detail means that your story won't come to life and the reader won't have enough information for their imagination to build on.

◆ Setting 1 – a market

Read Sources I and II on page 7. These are descriptions of markets. They come from two different historical novels. Both authors use details to build up an image of a Roman market held in the forum. They create a sense of place by the descriptions they use.

SOURCE I An extract from *Man Eater* by Marilyn Todd (1997). One of the characters, Quintilian, is crossing the forum in a town in southern Italy.

Being the third day of the Festival of Mars, the forum was packed to capacity. Butchers' cleavers splintered their blocks; mongrels plundered the scrap bins. Shouts of 'stop thief' or 'make way for the chariot' mingled with smells of pies and poultry, pickles and pancakes. A spice seller skidded on a fish head, and a thousand exotic scents exploded into the air. Cinnamon and nutmeg and cumin clung to Quintilian as he bumbled his way through the shoppers and the CHARLATANS. *You could buy anything here today from pastry cutters to ivory plaques, cucumbers to scribes.*

And the sun beat mercilessly on it all, pounding his head like a PESTLE.

SOURCE II An extract from *Two for the Lions* by Lindsey Davis (1998).

Beneath the kiosks' shade every kind of sale was being conducted on flat-topped stone tables, with the emphasis on domestic trade. Peas, lentils and other pulses were piled in dry heaps; figs and dates were set out on fruit stalls; both raw almonds and cakes made from almonds and honey were temptingly available. There were fish. There were cereals. It was the wrong time of year for grapes, but I saw vine leaves, both ready stuffed or strung together in brine to take home and stuff as you chose. Butchers, advertising with crude pictures of cows, pigs, camels and goats, were honing their knives on a lion footed bench in the weights and measures corner, while the weights and measures inspectors craned their necks over a hot game of draughts scratched on the ground.

There is a lot to see in each of these market scenes, but the things described are not just given to the reader in a long list. The extract from *Man Eater* uses some ALLITERATION to catch your attention. For example, 'A spice seller skidded on a fish head.' Source II uses short sentences so that you notice each different thing in turn. Both authors use strong VERBS to make their descriptions clearer and more vivid. Rather than write, 'a spice seller tripped on a fish head,' the author chose a verb that makes the action easier to picture in your head. The verb *plundered* in the phrase 'mongrels plundered the scrap bins' not only tells you what the dogs were doing but exactly how they did it – their antics were certainly not dainty or careful!

HOW TO WRITE

ACTIVITY

Look carefully at these descriptions of the two markets. On a copy of these sources:
1 Highlight in one colour examples of alliteration.
2 Highlight in another colour the verbs that you think bring these two places to life.
3 In a third colour highlight any information about the food that Romans ate.
4 Using the food clues in Source II, can you guess roughly where in the Roman Empire this town was? Explain your answer.

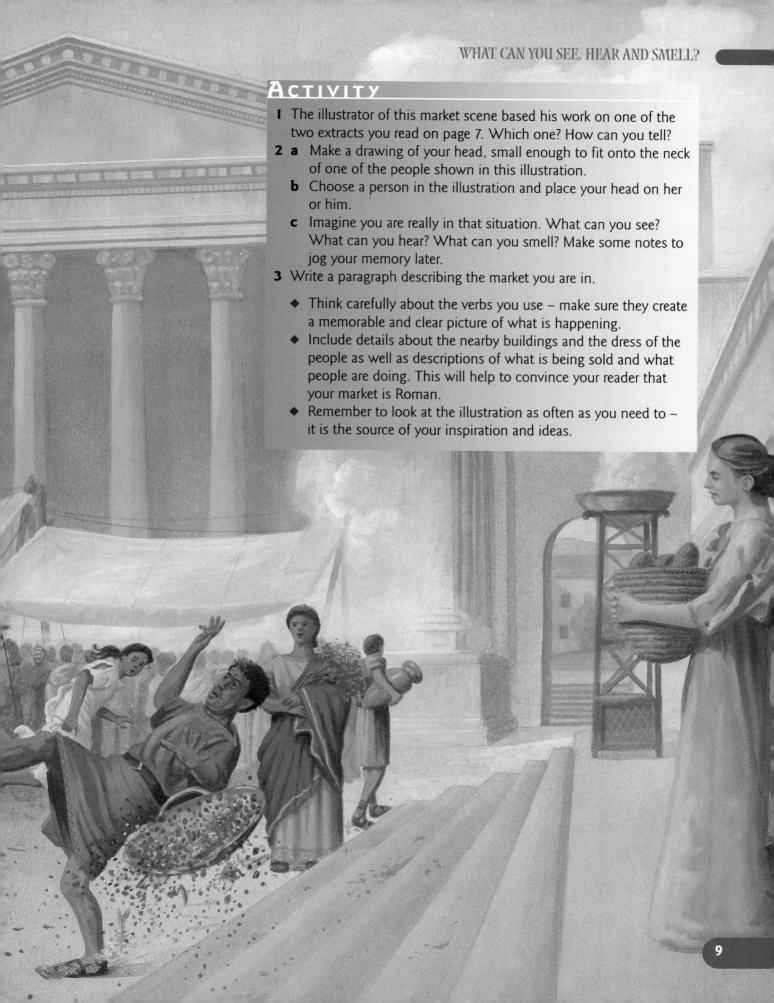

ACTIVITY

1 The illustrator of this market scene based his work on one of the two extracts you read on page 7. Which one? How can you tell?

2 **a** Make a drawing of your head, small enough to fit onto the neck of one of the people shown in this illustration.

    b Choose a person in the illustration and place your head on her or him.

    c Imagine you are really in that situation. What can you see? What can you hear? What can you smell? Make some notes to jog your memory later.

3 Write a paragraph describing the market you are in.

- Think carefully about the verbs you use – make sure they create a memorable and clear picture of what is happening.
- Include details about the nearby buildings and the dress of the people as well as descriptions of what is being sold and what people are doing. This will help to convince your reader that your market is Roman.
- Remember to look at the illustration as often as you need to – it is the source of your inspiration and ideas.

Setting 2 – a street

SOURCE I One of the 45 public drinking fountains in Pompeii.

Decorated water spout.

SOURCE II Graffiti found in Pompeii.

THE WEAVER SUCCESSUS LOVES
THE INNKEEPER'S SLAVE GIRL, IRIS BY NAME.
SHE DOESN'T CARE FOR HIM,
BUT HE BEGS HER TO TAKE PITY ON HIM.
WRITTEN BY HIS RIVAL. SO LONG.

SOURCE III Graffiti found in Pompeii.

A COPPER POT
IS MISSING
FROM THIS SHOP.
65 SESTERCES
REWARD
IF ANYBODY
BRINGS IT BACK,
20 SESTERCES IF
HE REVEALS THE
THIEF SO WE
CAN GET OUR
PROPERTY BACK.

SOURCE IV An extract from *Venus in Copper*, by Lindsey Davis (1991) where the narrator describes Abacus Street.

It was a tasteful thoroughfare, a single cart's width. The junction at one end had a well-kept public fountain; the other had a small street market, mainly kitchen pottery and vegetable stalls. In between, the shopkeepers washed and swept their own frontages; they were doing this at the hour I arrived, in a way I found pleasantly businesslike. Both sides of the street were lined with artisans' booths: cutlers, cheese shops, pickle sellers, cloth merchants, and locksmiths. Between each pair ran an entry with stairs to apartments above, and a passage to the ground-floor accommodation which lay behind the shops. The buildings were about three storeys high, brick-faced without balconies, though many had neat window boxes supported on brackets, while in other places rugs and counterpanes were already being given their daily airing over windowsills.

Background image: paving stones in Pompeii.

SOURCE V An illustration by Alan Sorrell of a street in Roman London. He was a well-known *ARCHÆOLOGIST* and illustrator. Each of his reconstruction drawings was based upon very careful research to ensure it was as accurate as possible.

SOURCE VI Extract from Juvenal's (*CIRCA* AD60–C. AD130) *Satires*. A *satire* is a piece of work that holds an aspect of behaviour or life up to scorn, using ridicule or irony.

However fast I hurry the crowd blocks my way and people behind tread on my heels. I get an elbow in the ribs. Then someone gives me a knock on the head from a plank or a barrel Everyone is treading on me. The streets are filthy, our legs are plastered with mud. If a wagon turns over and sheds its load of stone all over the passers-by, what's left of their bodies? Who will identify the remains?

ACTIVITY

Source IV is another example of how an author creates a sense of place within their story. All the details have been made specific to a time of day. In this scene, the character has clearly arrived at the start of what is going to be a busy morning and the people around are getting on with their work.

Use all the sources on these two pages to help you write another story setting based on the following idea:

It is early morning and you have just arrived in a Roman town. You have to try and make your way through its busy streets to the *forum*, where you have arranged to meet somebody outside the *basilica*. It is important that you are not late.

The paragraph you write must describe the things you see around you. It must also make it clear that you are in a hurry and that possibly you are quite anxious about the meeting.

When you write a story the action will probably happen in more than one place. You do not have to have a street scene in your story, but you could use this one. Whatever settings you decide to use, you need to think about each one and how to bring it to life in the imagination of your reader.

VICIOUS THUGS OR BRAVE WARRIORS?

Use the gingerbread technique to create believable characters

"It's all very well having a setting, but who are you going to write about? You need characters – and the *amphitheatre* is a good place to find some."

We learn about characters from how they behave in a situation. You don't need to explain that somebody in your story is bad tempered, you can show it through the way you describe what they do and say and how they do and say it ('she scowled, threw down the book and stamped out, slamming the door'). Use verbs that are descriptive, like *complained*, *snapped* or *shouted*, and choose ADVERBS that give a clear idea of how something was done, for example, *charmlessly*, *angrily*. Another way of adding detail to character is to use SIMILE to suggest comparisons. The authors of Sources I–III and V all use simile.

The description in Source I works well because the author uses a mixture of writing tricks to bring these two gladiators to life. There is a mixture of ADJECTIVES and similes that build up a picture of character. Strong descriptive verbs and adverbs add flesh to a character's bones. Then, just to show that, despite their appearance, these are gladiators not to be taken too seriously, the author of Source I uses phrases to undermine their 'tough guy' image. Look at phrases such as, 'smack themselves silly'.

SOURCE I Extract from *Venus in Copper* by Lindsey Davis (1991). The narrator is Marcus Didius Falco. He has just been released from prison but is about to be attacked by his landlord's gladiators.

Too late, I noticed a pair of disreputable bruisers posing against a PORTICO so that they could show off their muscles to anyone who had to pass on their side of the street. They wore loincloths, with leather strips tied round their knees and ankles to make them look tough. Their arrogance was horribly familiar.

"Oh look – it's Falco!"

"Oh COBNUTS – Rodan and Asiacus!"

Next moment one of them was behind me with his elbows clenched around my upper arms, while the other shook me charmlessly by the hand – a process which involved pulling out my wrist until my arm joints strained in their sockets like bowlines fighting their couplings on a GALLEY in a hurricane.

The smell of old sweat and recent garlic was bringing tears to my eyes.

"Oh cut it, Rodan, my reach is already long enough ..."

To call these two 'gladiators' insulted even the clapped out hulks who usually feature in that trade. Rodan and Asiacus trained at a barracks which was run by my landlord Smaractus, and when they were not smacking themselves silly with practice swords he sent them out to make the streets even more dangerous than usual. They never did much work in the arena; their role in public life was to intimidate the unfortunate tenants who rented homes from him. For me, being in prison had had one great advantage: avoiding my landlord, and these pet thugs of his.

SOURCE II Extract from *The Mark of the Horse Lord* by Rosemary Sutcliff (1965). The gladiators are sitting waiting in a room below the arena. They are going to take part in a show where the individual duels are to be to the death.

A forceful step sounded in the corridor, and the Captain of the Gladiators appeared in the dark entry. He stood an instant looking down at them.

"Time to helm-up, lads."

Phaedrus got to his feet with the rest, catching up his plumed helmet from the bench beside him, and stepped forward from his dark corner. The light from the nearest lamp showed him naked like the other sword fighters, save for the belted leather loin guard and the sleeve of supple bronze hoop-mail on his sword arm; a young man with hair the colour of hot copper, lithe and hollow flanked as a yearling wolf, the tanned pallor of his face slashed across by red brows and reckless, faintly smiling mouth.

He put on the heavy helmet and buckled the chin-strap. Now he was seeing the world through the long eye slits in the moulded mask, and thought, testing the buckle,

"My last sight of the world will be like this, looking out at it sharp-edged and bright from the darkness inside my helmet."

And then he pushed the thought away. It wasn't lucky to have that kind of thought, going into the arena. That was the way one's nerve began to go.

ACTIVITY

1 Read Sources I–III and V carefully (III and V are on the next page). These are writers' descriptions of five very different gladiators. Match the descriptions to the illustrations below by a modern artist. Who is missing?

2 Choose one character from Sources II, III or V. How does the author bring the character to life? On your own copy of the source, highlight the verbs you think are particularly effective at creating a sense of character. Highlight any similes that the author uses.

3 Look at the illustrations of the gladiators or of any of the other people you have met so far in this book. Write two similes to describe their characters.

SOURCE III Extract from *A Murder on the Appian Way* by Steven Saylor (1996). The narrator, Gordianus, describes the gladiator who has come to his town house to escort him safely to a meeting with Pompey the Great.

He was a big man, probably a gladiator or a soldier, despite the richly embroidered fabric of his grey tunic and dark green cape. His nose had been broken, maybe more than once, and each of his hands was the size of a baby's head. His own head was as bald as a baby's, and almost as ugly. He had the look of a man who could walk through a dangerous place without being bothered.

"Who sent you ... citizen?" I said, noting the iron ring on his finger. He was probably someone's FREEDMAN.

"The Great One," he said bluntly. His voice was like gravel in a sluice.

Baby Face and his troop of gladiators closed around us like an armoured tortoise for the walk down the Ramp, across the forum and through the Fontinalis Gate.

SOURCE IV A still from the film *Gladiator* (2000) showing Maximus in the arena.

SOURCE V Extract from *Two for the Lions* by Lindsey Davis (1998). Marcus Didius Falco, the narrator, has arrived to interview Rumex as part of an enquiry into the death of a man-eating lion.

There was a small knock on the door, then a slave opened it for Rumex. I knew as soon as I saw him that I might as well have not bothered.

He had probably been stupid before but fighting had made him worse. He was tall, lithe on his feet, beautifully honed in the body, hideous ugly in the features, and as dense as a wharfside pile. He could probably string two words together – if they were 'where's mine?', 'get lost' or 'kill him'. That was his limit. He walked into his master's room as if he was afraid of knocking over furniture, yet the dance in his feet that must make him the envy of his opponents was obvious even here. He was definitely powerful and looked as if he could be fearless too.

There was a rather silly fringe on his tunic skirt, and he wore a gold necklace that must have cost a fortune though its design was of astounding trashiness.

ACTIVITY

Sometimes writers use a technique called *gingerbreading* to help them develop their ideas for a character. All the physical qualities are written around the outside of the figure. All of the qualities of personality are written inside. Look at the gingerbread figure below for the gladiator Rumex, from Source V.

You are going to use this gingerbread technique to help you create your own gladiator character. You could use this character later in your story, but if you don't, this is a good technique for you to learn for when you develop your own characters. Use either the gingerbread sheet given to you by your teacher or else draw a basic gingerbread figure like the one opposite. For your gladiator, decide:

◆ on his physical appearance
◆ on his age
◆ what sort of person he is (look at the inside of the Rumex gingerbread as an example)
◆ where he is (this will affect what he is wearing and how he is behaving).

Now, using Sources IV and VI–VIII and your gingerbread figure to help you, write your own description of a gladiator who may appear in your story. Remember that gladiators were usually slaves or criminals, although occasionally freemen chose to fight in the arena. The gladiators in the descriptions are very different and this is partly to do with where they are. Phaedrus is in the arena. Rodan and Asiacus are in the street and Rumex is in his master's house.

When you have finished your gingerbread gladiator you might like to illustrate him.

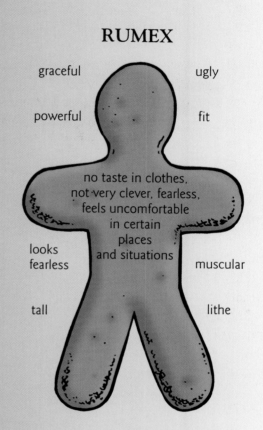

RUMEX

graceful   ugly

powerful   fit

no taste in clothes, not very clever, fearless, feels uncomfortable in certain places and situations

looks fearless   muscular

tall   lithe

SOURCE VI   Types of gladiator.

A **retarius** fought with a net and TRIDENT with armour on the forearms.

A **myrmillo** fought with a curved sword, small shield, helmet with a fish-shaped crest and light armour.

A **samnite** fought with a straight sword, large oblong shield and heavy armour.

A **thracian** fought with a sword or dagger, and a round shield.

SOURCE VII A gladiator's helmet found at Herculaneum. The fish crest shows it was worn by a Myrmillo who would have fought a Retarius.

SOURCE VIII Mosaic from Curium. In this mosaic, the gladiator Lytras fighting as a Myrmillo is shown about to kill his opponent, but the referee Darios stops him. The other officials who would be in the arena were Rhadamanthus, Lord of the Underworld, wearing a beaked mask and carrying a ceremonial mallet with which he claimed the dead, and Hermes, messenger of the Gods, who carried a red hot CADUCEUS to check that the gladiators were indeed dead and not just faking.

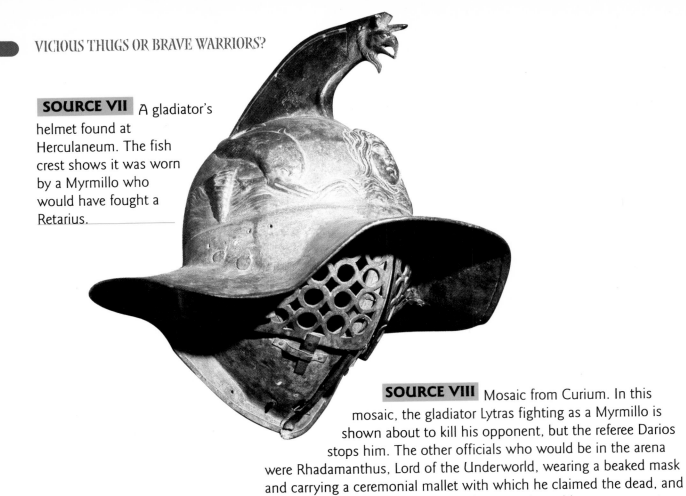

SOURCE IX Graffiti scratched on a wall in Pompeii.

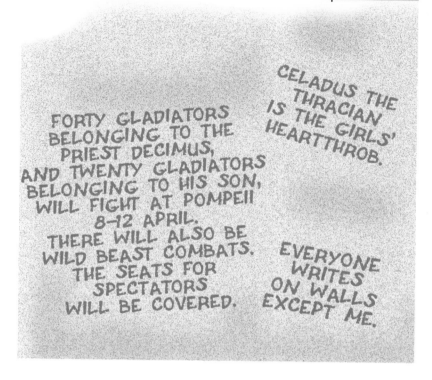

FORTY GLADIATORS BELONGING TO THE PRIEST DECIMUS, AND TWENTY GLADIATORS BELONGING TO HIS SON, WILL FIGHT AT POMPEII 8–12 APRIL. THERE WILL ALSO BE WILD BEAST COMBATS. THE SEATS FOR SPECTATORS WILL BE COVERED.

CELADUS THE THRACIAN IS THE GIRLS' HEARTTHROB.

EVERYONE WRITES ON WALLS EXCEPT ME.

SOURCE XI Extract from the writings of Tacitus, *c.* AD120.

What is it that young people talk about at home and at school? Actors, horses and gladiators.

SOURCE X A modern artist's reconstruction of the Roman amphitheatre of Durnovaria (present-day Dorchester). The artist's interpretation is based on the known archaeological evidence.

SOURCE XII The Roman writer Seneca's comments on gladiatorial shows, *c.* AD55.

I reached the arena at lunchtime, expecting there to be a pause in the slaughter and hoping for fun and relaxation. But not a bit of it. In the morning criminals had been thrown to the lions. Now they were forced to fight each other. When a man killed another he was then killed by the next. The crowd loved it. 'Kill him! Lash him! Burn him!' they shouted. 'Why does that one give in easily? Give him a taste of the whip, that'll make him fight!' Not a moment is lost. The killing goes on and on all day long.

"It's all very well having a setting and some characters, but what are they going to do? You need to have a plot."

SOURCE I The front cover of *The Guard Dog Geese* by Mick Gowar (1997).

All good adventure stories begin with a **problem**. Perhaps something goes wrong for the main characters or perhaps something happens that forces them to take action. Part of the excitement of the story comes from the way the characters resolve that problem and from the way their experiences affect and change them. The important events that happen on the way to resolving the problem are called **conflicts**.

Here is part of the plot of *The Guard Dog Geese* by Mick Gowar. Because this story is for younger children, aged about seven to ten, it has a simple plot with a believable problem to start the action off. Here it is:

Livia, a young Roman girl, and her family have come from Britain to live with Great Uncle Titus in his VILLA outside Rome. Bored by country life, Livia has been promised a trip to Ostia, the port, to visit the family warehouses and the baths.

Unfortunately, Great Uncle Titus is very superstitious and the day of the trip happens to be a bad luck day. He cancels the trip and declares that nobody can leave the house until a HARUSPEX – a priest who examines the ENTRAILS of animal sacrifices for omens from the gods – has sacrificed and declared the bad luck over. This proves the last straw for Livia. Despite the instruction to stay indoors, she leaves the villa to explore.

You can see the problem set up at the start of this story. The main character is bored and lonely, and when her hoped-for outing is cancelled, things only get worse. However, this problem is not quite enough to make a good story, it needs the addition of the head of the household ordering that nobody can go outside until the bad luck has passed. Once this order has been given, the possibilities for all sorts of trouble and adventure are enormous. The plot continues like this:

Once Livia leaves the villa, she explores the farmyard, hoping to find the five-legged piglet that has caused the bad luck day. Before she has gone too far, the farm geese, used by Romans as feathered guard dogs, chase her. This is the first conflict to arise out of the problem. The second conflict is that, as she runs away from the geese, Livia finds the ground giving way beneath her and she falls into what appears to be a small cave. This adds a further complication to the story. Now she is outside – on her own – and trapped below ground with an injured leg.

This story is eventually resolved when Livia's nurse alerts the family to her disappearance. The honking of the geese guides them to Livia. So, the geese, who put her in danger, turn out to be Livia's rescuers in the end.

Story problems featuring some people you have already met

Lytras, the gladiator, is sitting in the theatre at Curium, saving a seat for his master. As he is sitting quietly waiting, the man next to him suddenly clutches his throat and falls to the floor. Lytras hears the unfortunate man gasp the word 'poison'.

Paulina, the baker's wife, goes to the market in Pompeii with Marcia, one of her house slaves. Suddenly and quite unexpectedly, Marcia grabs an amber necklace from the jeweller's stall and runs off into the crowd.

Agrippa is a wilful boy who is in a hurry to grow up and make his mark on the world. His father, Petronius, takes him to the *amphitheatre* in Durnovaria to watch the games. While Petronius talks to a friend, Agrippa sneaks off to get a look at the gladiators before the action starts. At first his father is not worried and expects him to return for the end of the games. As time passes and the boy is nowhere to be seen, his father begins to panic. Where is Agrippa and what is he doing?

ACTIVITY

You are going to develop a plot line from an initial problem.

1 Look at the four story problems below and choose one.
2 Either on your own or with a partner, think about how the problem you have chosen could be developed into a story or narrative. Record your ideas as you go and then make a flow diagram of your plot line. Your teacher may show you a flow diagram of the plot of *The Guard Dog Geese* as an example of how to set out a plot flow diagram.
3 When you have created your plot line, add notes to the different stages with ideas for making the Roman setting clear.

Silvia has come to the baths in Lectis Magna. While she is changing in the APODYTERIA, she finds a wax tablet with a message inscribed on it. A quick reading of the message tells her that there is a conspiracy against the Emperor. One of the conspirators named is none other than the Emperor's younger son, Domitian. Silvia must decide what she is going to do about her find.

Three things to keep in mind

◆ The plot is the key to a successful story. It must contain ideas that fire the reader's imagination. The plot is the thing that lingers in the imagination after the story has ended.

◆ In an historical story, the historical period puts limits on what can and cannot happen in your story. In a Roman story, you can't include anything that the Romans did not have or did not do.

◆ Remember to use the illustrations, sources and information in this book to help you think of plot lines for your Roman story.

THE LUCK OF THE DRAW

Collect settings, characters and problems to improvise a story

How to play 'The luck of the draw'

I Your aim is to collect a complete story set of two 'Character cards', one 'Setting card' and one 'Problem card'.

II Play the game with a partner.

III You will need a dice, a playing piece for each player and a set of game cards.

IV Throw the dice to decide who goes first.

V Throw the dice again and move your playing piece the number of squares it shows. Move around the board following the instructions on each square.

VI When you land on a character, setting or problem square, you can take a card. If you already have enough of that type of card then do nothing.

VII The winner is the first person to make a complete story set. You may need to go round the board several times to do this.

VIII The other player then picks up the cards they need to complete their story set without moving around the board.

After the game: tell your story

IX Next, you and your partner need to make up two stories, one for each complete story card set. Each of your stories should bring together the four cards in each story set. You may want to compare your stories with the stories of other people in your class.

Improve the game

X Now that you have played the game through and made up your own stories, you are ready to improve the game. Make your own character, setting and problem cards using your knowledge of the Romans.

Play it again

XI Finally, swap your new cards with another pair and play the game again.

XII What stories can you make up this time? Which is your favourite?

XIII Be ready to narrate your favourite story to the rest of the class.

Miss a turn

Pick up a Character card

Pick up a Problem card

Pick up a Problem card

THE LUCK OF THE DRAW

Choose any card you wish

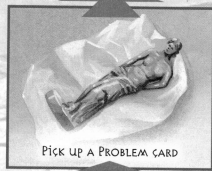

Browse in the Imperial Library looking for possible story ideas

Pick up a Setting card

Pick up a Character card

Pick up a Character card

START

Pick up a Setting card

Give back one card

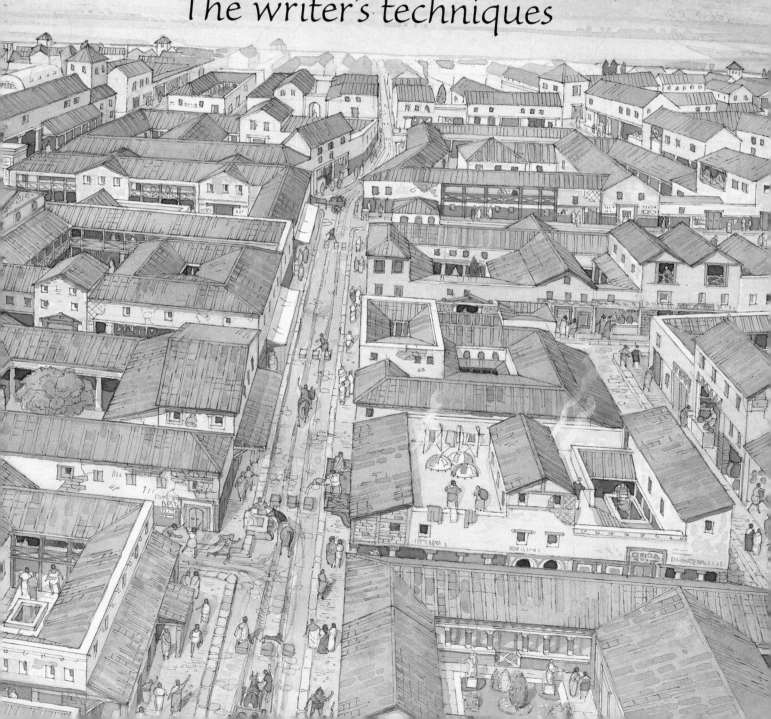

SECTION 2

WRITING YOUR STORY
The writer's techniques

"So, you've got a setting and some characters and you've got a plot; now how are you going to begin your story? What you need is a good story opening!"

The beginning of a story is the most important part: if you don't grab the reader's attention within the first few sentences, they won't read on. There are a number of ways of opening a story and you need to think about what the opening of a story does.

The first paragraphs of your story will set the scene for the action. They will also introduce one or more characters and present the problem around which your story is built. Once you have decided on these, you can think about the process of writing.

The first words on the page are always difficult, but it helps to have mastered a few writer's tricks. The next few sections will teach you some techniques to grab the reader's attention in the first few lines of your story.

◆ Story openings using dialogue

The first type of story opening uses DIALOGUE. Beginning a story with dialogue is a good way of introducing characters. It doesn't need lots of descriptive NARRATIVE but lets you suggest what a character is like through what they say and how they react. Look at this opening to the novel *Last Act in Palmyra* by Lindsey Davis (1994).

> *"Somebody could get killed here!" Helena exclaimed.*
> *I grinned, watching the arena avidly. "That's what we're meant to be hoping for!" Playing the bloodthirsty spectator comes easily to a Roman.*
> *"I'm worried about the elephant," she murmured.*

This opening from the Lindsey Davis novel shows two characters who clearly know each other well and who are used to teasing each other. It also gives the reader information about where the characters are (setting) and what they are doing.

For a dialogue story opening you need to visualise your characters very clearly before you start writing. What kind of people are they? What do they do? How do they behave towards each other? For this style of writing the rule is: paint a word portrait – have a strong mental picture of what your characters are like.

◆ *Story openings using action*

Some stories start with action. This kind of story opening has a Latin name, *IN MEDIAS RES*, which, literally translated, means 'in the middle of things'. The writer takes the reader straight into the action of a story without having introduced the characters, the problem or even the setting first. It is an excellent way of creating a hook to hold the reader's attention, making them want to read on. Here are some examples:

> **Example A**
> And then Florianus clamped his hand over the dice. He said in a voice as soft as silk, 'Has nobody ever told you that it is usual to pay a gambling debt before leaving the table?'
>
> **Example B**
> Suddenly I heard it. There, in the darkness and the almost silence, something moved. Though slight, the sound was unmistakable, especially to someone who remembered only too well where she had heard it before.
>
> **Example C**
> Time seemed to stop. The crowd held its breath as the gladiator fell.

The way these sentences are written helps to create an impression of tension or drama. The first example begins the sentence with the CONJUNCTION 'and'. By starting a sentence with a conjunction, you focus the reader's attention on what follows. The same is true for beginning a sentence with an adverb like 'suddenly'. The final example uses short, simple sentences to build up the tension of the scene.

ACTIVITY B

Practise writing a story opening using action.

1 Try using the structure of Example A which starts with the conjunction 'And'. Here is another example that uses the same structure:
'And then Paulina broke the loaf apart. Embedded in the freshly baked dough was the missing necklace.'

Now try writing two or three examples of your own.

2 Write some story openings modelled on Example B. Here is another example that follows the same structure:
'Suddenly the room was plunged into darkness. From behind him, Lucius heard the sound of a door being locked.'

3 Now try writing the opening sentences to your story using the style of Example C. Remember that *in medias res* introduces the characters and the setting through the action.

◆ *Story openings using setting – the laundry*

SILVIA

> It's lovely to see you again. I'll take you to the public baths for some pampering. First, though, I need to go via the laundry to collect my husband's TOGA. We're holding an important CENA tonight and he needs to look his best.

SOURCE I The laundry of Stephanus at Pompeii showing vats for bleaching cloth using urine. This was one of 18 laundries in the town.

SOURCE II Extract from *The Silver Pigs* by Lindsey Davis. Marcus Didius Falco, the narrator, describes a laundry run by Lenia, the washerwoman, which is on the ground floor of a tenement building.

We pushed through the wet garments Lenia was allowing to dry out in the street, turning our faces away as they flapped back at us, then went in.

Lenia's laundry. Steam billowed out to flatten us. Washerboys stamped the clothes, sploshing up to their cracked little knees in hot tubs. There was a great deal of noise – slapping the linen, thumping and pounding it, clanging cauldrons – all in a close, echoing atmosphere. The laundry took up the whole ground floor, spilling out into the courtyard at the back.

'Tinkle into the bucket before you take her up', Lenia said.

I shall have to explain about the bucket and the bleach vat ...

They do use carbonate of soda, FULLER'S EARTH and pipeclay for the brilliant robes of election candidates. But the pristine togas of our magnificent Empire are effectively bleached with urine, obtained from the public latrines. The Emperor Vespasian, never slow to light on brisk new ways of squeezing out cash, had slapped a tax on this ancient trade in human waste. Lenia paid the tax, though on principle she increased her supply for nothing whenever she could.

Look at the second paragraph of Source II. Lindsey Davis has painted a vivid picture of Lenia's laundry. It sets the scene for the conversation between the two characters. It could be the start of your story. Stories can begin with this sort of descriptive scene setting. When you write in this way you concentrate on how things look, how things sound and how things smell before you introduce an action or a character.

SOURCE III Shell fish called Purpura. The Romans made a dye from these which they used to dye the purple stripe in the *togas* of emperors and all other Romans of rank.

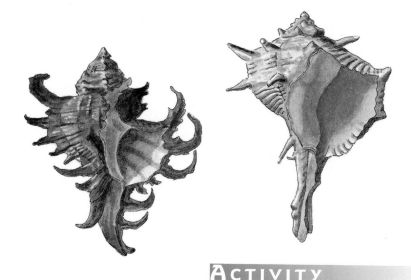

ACTIVITY

Now write an opening paragraph using setting. You could use this laundry or you could choose any of the many different settings in this book.

Don't worry about the smell, it's just the urine. That reminds me of the story about Emperor Vespasian that I heard yesterday. You know he put a tax on urine? Well, when his son Titus complained about the tax, Vespasian held a copper under his nose and asked him if it smelt!

WHAT WILL YOUR CHARACTERS SAY TO EACH OTHER?

Play knucklebones and visit a *thermopolium* to find out how to write good dialogue

"You may or may not have decided to open your story with dialogue, but you will need to write dialogue somewhere in your story. The most likely place will be where several characters meet together, such as in a bar."

SOURCE I A set of knucklebones and dice.

SOURCE II A mosaic of dice players.

The rules of Knucklebones (or TALI)

Knucklebones was a very popular Roman game. It was played with four *tali*, originally made from the knucklebones of sheep or goats. Each *tali* could land on one of four sides with the values 1, 3, 4 or 6. The mosaic, Source II, shows how the *tali* were marked. Rules varied. The scoring in the table on the right is based on simple numerical superiority, except for Venus, Senio, Vultures, and Dogs (lowest of the Vultures). In the case of equal scores, poker-like rules would be used. So a triple beats a pair, but two pairs beat a triple. More advanced players could adapt other poker-like rules.

SCORING RULES FOR KNUCKLEBONES:

(1,3,4,6): *Venus* – all four *tali* showing a different side.
(6,6,6,4): Total = 22
(6,6,6,3): Total = 21
(6,6,4,4): Total = 20
(6,6,6,1): Total = 19 (high)
(6,6,4,3): Total = 19
(6,6,3,3): Total = 18
(6,6,4,1): Total = 17
(6,6,3,1): Total = 16
(4,4,4,3): Total = 15
(6,6,1,1): Total = 14 (high)
(4,4,3,3): Total = 14
(4,4,4,1): Total = 13
(4,4,3,1): Total = 12

(4,3,3,1): Total = 11
(4,4,1,1): Total = 10 (high)
(3,3,3,1): Total = 10
(4,3,1,1): Total = 9
(3,3,1,1): Total = 8
(4,1,1,1): Total = 7
(3,1,1,1): Total = 6
(6,x,x,x): *Senio* – a single six and anything
(6,6,6,6): *Vultures* – all four *tali* the same
(4,4,4,4): *Vultures* – all four *tali* the same
(3,3,3,3): *Vultures* – all four *tali* the same
(1,1,1,1): *Dogs* – lowest of the Vultures

ACTIVITY A

1 Make a set of *tali*. You could do this by taking an ordinary dice and covering and renumbering four of the sides, or by marking four sides of a pencil. If a blank side comes up then just throw that *tali* again. Better still, mark the squared end of a chopstick. The four sides should be numbered 1, 3, 4, and 6. You could use Roman numerals but this does make it a little more difficult when you play.

2 Find two other people to play with and you are ready to play a game of Knucklebones. Each player throws the *tali* and checks their score against the scoring chart to see who wins that round (highest wins). The overall winner is the person who wins most rounds out of nine. Remember (and this is very important), enjoy the game, but also think about what the three of you say to each other during your game, because this will help you later. Alternatively, your teacher might suggest you observe another group as they play.

ACTIVITY B

1 Now you are going to use these ideas to help you to write some dialogue between three Roman Knucklebone players. Source II shows three Roman men playing dice in a bar, but any Roman, male or female, might have played either game anywhere. Decide who is playing and where. Give your characters names. You might use some of the characters you have already developed.

2 Write a simple conversation that might start with talking about the game, but then moves on to other things. Simply record who says what. Remember to use speech marks and start a new line each time the speaker changes.

3 Put in some REPORTING CLAUSES to identify exactly who is speaking. You don't need to do this for every line of speech, just often enough for the reader to keep up with who is doing the talking.

4 Pay attention to the verbs you use in the reporting clause. Don't rely on words like 'said' and 'replied'. Consider how the characters speak to one another. You could discuss the alternatives to the word 'said' – it would be handy to have a THESAURUS. If you do use simple verbs like 'said' and 'replied' include an adverb like 'angrily' or 'urgently' to give some clue about how the words were spoken.

5 Add some lines of descriptive narrative. This means interrupt the dialogue with a description of what one character was doing or thinking as the dialogue was spoken. This will also make the setting clear.

6 When you have finished, read your work through. Does your dialogue give a sense of the characters as real people?

◆ Using dialogue to develop your plot – a thermopolium

ACTIVITY A

Study Sources I and II.
1 What similarities can you find between each THERMOPOLIUM in these two sources?
2 How does the author of Source I bring her *thermopolium* to life?

SOURCE I An extract from *Poseidon's Gold* by Lindsey Davis (1993). Marcus Didius Falco, the narrator, describes Flora's, a *thermopolium*.

It squatted on the corner where a dingy lane down from the Aventine met a dirty track up from the wharves. It had the usual arrangement, with two counters set at right angles for people in the two streets to lean on reflectively while they waited to be poisoned. The counters were made from a rough patchwork of white and grey stone that a man might mistake for marble if his mind was on the elections and he was nearly blind. Each counter had three circular holes to take cauldrons of food. At Flora's most of the holes were left empty, out of respect for public health perhaps. What the full cauldrons held was even more disgusting than the usual brown sludge with funny specks in it that's ladled out to passers-by from rotten street food shops. Flora's cold potages were off-puttingly lukewarm, and their hot meats were dangerously cool.

The counters enclosed a cramped square space where really hardened regulars could sit down and have their ears knocked by the waiter's elbow as he went about his work. There were two sagging tables; one had benches, the other a set of folding campstools.

SOURCE II The remains of a *thermopolium* in Pompeii. Warm or cold food would be stored in covered jars kept warm in the holes in the counter – dishes like peas, beans, lentils, soups and meat stews. Wine would be kept cool in storage jars in another counter. There were more than 200 varieties of wine to choose from. Non-alcoholic drinks such as fruit juices would also be available. Customers would be served by the waiter, often a slave, and would either eat and drink standing in the street or sit at tables by the counter.

SOURCE III An extract from *Outpost Fortress*, a short story by Rosemary Sutcliff (1973). Lucius, the narrator, is describing a dice game he was playing in.

... I was casting the dice with Florianus. I had Ahriman the Black One's luck that night.

Again and again I threw the Dog, the lowest throw of all, while Florianus' luck was as far in as mine was out. It was fortunate – very fortunate for me that night – that along the frontiers, where few of us had more than our pay to live on, we seldom played for high stakes. But I could not remember that evening's play more vividly if we had been dicing for a kingdom. I remember Florianus' face in the lamplight, smiling a little, with narrowed eyes, and the rattle of the dice in the wooden cup, and his hand spilling out fours and fives and sixes across the wine soaked table.

I don't know how long we played, but it must have been a good while later that he made the final throw of the game, and laughed softly. 'Aha! Venus!'

'Shall we play again?'

'Not tonight,' I said. 'You've about cleaned me out.'

He gave a small shrug. 'How sad! And I had a feeling your luck was just on the turn.'

I looked at the three sixes lying on the table, and they seemed to stare back at me with all their eighteen malicious little black eyes. 'I'm afraid I've lost count. How much do I owe you?'

'Not much. Six hundred sesterces I make it.'

I had indeed lost count – oh, it wasn't very much! Less than half the price of a good native pony or an untrained slave. At the start of the month, I could have paid it and got through till next payday by tightening my belt. But it was near the end of the month, and my purse was low.

I was ashamed. I said: 'I'm sorry. I can give you two now, and the rest next week when I get my pay.'

He said in a voice as soft as silk, 'Has no one ever told you that it is usual to pay a gambling debt before leaving the table?'

ACTIVITY B

Read Source III. What happens next?

Get into a group of four. You are now going to practise using dialogue to develop your plot. You are going to take part in a role-play exercise based on the events in Source III.

One person should take the part of each of the following four characters:

◆ Lucius
◆ Florianus
◆ a slave waiter
◆ Antonius, a friend of Lucius.

First of all, discuss what might happen next. How will Lucius resolve his problem so that he can leave the *thermopolium* safely? Then improvise what happens next. Start your role play at the point where Florianus throws a Venus.

SOURCE IV

WHO WILL BE YOUR STORY TELLER?
Work out the advantages and disadvantages of first person narrative

If you decide that one of the characters in your story is also going to be the narrator (the person who tells the story), then you will need to use first person narrative. This means that you will use the pronouns 'I', 'we', 'us' and 'my', etc., when telling the story. A very famous novel, *I, Claudius* by Robert Graves, uses this style of narrative. This is how Graves begins.

> *I, TIBERIUS CLAUDIUS DRUSUS NERO GERMANICUS This-that-and-the-other (for I shall not trouble you yet with all my titles), who was once, and not so long ago either, known to my friends and relatives and associates as 'Claudius the Idiot', or 'That Claudius', or 'Claudius the Stammerer', or 'Clau-Clau-Claudius', or at best as 'Poor Uncle Claudius', am now about to write this strange history of my life; starting from my earliest childhood and continuing year by year until I reach that fateful point of change where, some eight years ago, at the age of fifty-one, I found myself caught in what I may call the 'golden predicament' from which I have never since become disentangled.*

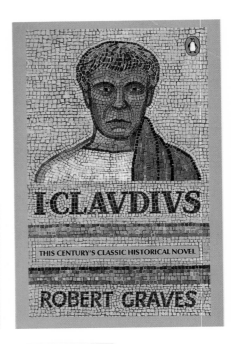

SOURCE 1   Robert Graves' classic novel *I, Claudius* was set in Roman times.

This book was written in 1934 and some of the sentence constructions used by Graves are unfamiliar to readers today. However, Graves still uses a hook to catch the reader by the way he makes his character speak and by the clues the character gives about the story to follow. The opening works because it sets up a character who is unlike the usual storybook hero: he stammers and people call him names. Then it hints that something extraordinary happens to him. Graves uses three key phrases to create questions in your mind about this man Claudius: 'this strange history of my life' (Why is it strange?); 'that fateful point of change' (If it was fateful, then clearly something very important happened. What was it?); and finally, 'I found myself caught in … the golden predicament' (A predicament means you are faced with difficult choices, but if it's also golden, then it sounds as if, on the surface at least, it's a predicament most people would want to find themselves in.).

Telling a story in the first person is very common in writing for children or young people. If it is done well it can be very gripping and easy to read. It has one important advantage: it lets you stop the narrative and speak directly to the reader whenever you want to. However, it also has a disadvantage. The danger is that you end up presenting everything from the point of view of one character – the narrator. It can then become very difficult to include all the details of the story, because we can only know what the narrator knows. If you choose this style of narrative for your work, you need to remember to describe the actions of other characters in detail. You will also need to make a point of slowing the action down from time to time so you can look around and let your reader see through your eyes.

This style of writing still needs you to set the scene and introduce the problem that will drive the narrative along. Robert Graves does this very well, but his paragraph is the opening to a very long novel. You will be able to establish your setting, character and problem much more quickly – even in the first sentence. You do it all the time when you talk about things that have happened to you. If you imagine yourself to be Lytras, who was waiting at the theatre for his master when a man collapsed beside him (see page 19), how would you begin to tell your fellow slaves about it? You'd probably say something like, 'Well, there I was, hanging around waiting for the boss to turn up at the theatre, when all of a sudden this man clutches his throat and falls to the floor gasping, "Poison!"' This will certainly hook your listener into wanting more details. As a writer, you can go on to provide more information and to describe the scene so that your readers feel they were there with you.

SOURCE II A dramatic mask decorates the theatre at Ostia.

SOURCE III This Roman terracotta lamp is decorated with gladiators fighting.

ACTIVITY

You are going to practise writing in the first person. You may want to use this technique for your story.
1 Study the four diaries on pages 34 and 35 and choose one of the characters.
2 Think about one part of that character's day that might have been significant. You have been given the bare bones of what happened that day. It is up to you to supply the interesting action. You could use the character's speech bubble to help you. Limit yourself to one incident only.
3 Write about the incident as if you were that character. Remember that even though you are writing about only one incident, you must describe the action carefully. Make sure you use verbs that are descriptive and that help your readers to create a picture of the action in their own imaginations.

◆ Telling the time

Romans relied on water clocks and sundials to tell the time. The day lasted as long as the daylight and was divided into twelve equal parts (HORAE). Midday was in the middle of the day, at the end of the sixth and start of the seventh hour.

There was terrible trouble at the tavern today.

Petronius' diary

First hour: IENTCULUM. A simple meal of lentils and apples.

Second hour: Supervise slaves on farm ditch digging.

Fourth hour: Ride into Durnovaria to visit mosaic workshop.

Sixth hour: Eat PRANDIUM in the tavern with friends.

Seventh hour: Return home to farm.

Ninth hour: Cena. Simple meal of smoked sausages and bread prepared by Vera, my slave cook.

Tenth hour: To bed.

Silvia's diary

First hour: Ientculum. A simple meal of figs and grapes.

Third hour: Receive visit from mother and sister.

Fifth hour: Consultation with Hanno, my slave cook, on the menu for tonight's cena, followed by a prandium of soft-boiled eggs, cheese and cucumber.

Sixth hour: Attend the ceremony at the Temple of Juno.

Seventh hour: Visit to the baths after checking on the laundry.

Ninth hour: Welcome guests as they arrive.

CENA
GUSTATIO Oysters with salads
MULSUM Fried mullet with prawns in a fish sauce
MENSA PRIMA Roast venison with leeks, served with fresh cabbage, beans, and sprouts
MENSA SECUNDA Honey cakes, stuffed dates, nuts, and apples, pears and grapes
All served with a selection of wines
Entertainment provided by Egyptian dancing girls and acrobats.

Eleventh hour: Farewell to dinner guests. To bed with husband.

What a dilemma! I didn't know what to do when I found that wax tablet.

Paulina's diary

First hour: *Ientculum*. A simple meal of bread and grapes.

Second hour: Working on accounts in the PISTRINA.

Fourth hour: Walk to the market in the forum, with my slave, Marcia, to carry purchases.

Sixth hour: *Prandium* of broad beans at home.

Seventh hour: Supervise Apicus, my slave cook, in his preparations for *cena* and the rest of my house slaves in their cleaning and the maintenance of my garden.

Ninth hour: *Cena* of stuffed kidneys and honeyed mushrooms with red wine.

Eleventh hour: To bed with husband.

> What a day! I had terrible trouble with my slave, Marcia, at the market …

Lytras' diary

First hour: *Ientculum*. A simple meal of bread and grapes.

Second hour: Training fight as a Myrmillo against a Retarius.

Fourth hour: Resting.

Sixth hour: *Prandium* of lentils at the gladiators' barracks.

Seventh hour: Sent to the theatre to save a seat for my master.

Eighth hour: Return to barracks for fitness training.

Ninth hour: *Cena* of *pulmentum*.

Tenth hour: To bed in sleeping cell.

> You'll never guess what happened when I was at the theatre!

... AND THEY ALL LIVED HAPPILY EVER AFTER!

Five better ways to end a story – which will you choose?

"You know how to open a story. You know how to develop a plot. You know how to describe characters and settings. But can you finish well? Will you tie all those loose ends together? These pages should help you to write a good ending to your story."

How you end a story is as important as how you begin it: the ending used in our title is very dull and boring. Your reader doesn't want to be disappointed. The problem that started the story off needs to be resolved, too. This is why story endings are called resolutions – they recognise the problem, sort it out and bring it to a close. Here are some tips on writing a good story ending once the problem has been resolved.

◆ Ending 1: *the lesson*

In many stories, especially adventure stories, the characters are often changed by their experiences. This doesn't just mean a change in their fortunes or their circumstances; the things that happen to them during the story make them see things differently. The characters learn from their experiences and have their opinions changed. They usually end up wiser, better people.

This means that you can choose to end your story by reflecting on what has happened to your main characters. *The Guard Dog Geese* by Mick Gowar provides a good example of this sort of reflective ending. The story ends with Drusilla, mother of Livia, thinking about what has happened and coming to the conclusion that they don't need an old-fashioned *haruspex*. What they do need is the up-to-date equivalent, an astrologer.

> Drusilla let out a quiet sigh of irritation. 'More old-fashioned nonsense!' she thought. 'When I get to Ostia,' she promised herself, 'I'm going to find a good astrologer. It's ridiculous to try and run a big household like this without an astrologer,' she thought. 'Almost like running it without a cook!'

◆ Ending 2: *the 'long shot'*

Another way of ending a story, once all the problems have been resolved, is to move away from your characters, showing them within their setting, getting on with their lives without you, the story teller, and looking forward to the future. Henry Treece's novel, *Legions of the Eagle*, does this.

> *There was nothing for it. Gaius had to laugh too. 'Come on,' he said, 'or this lot will get me into trouble!' Then he gave the order and they all began to move across the bridge. And as they went, the little dog frisked round the heels of the stern-faced soldier, and the last rays of the Gallic sun fell across the broad river, turning its blue currents to a rich red gold. Tomorrow, it seemed, would be a good day.*

A way to think of this type of ending is to imagine your story as a film. In the final moments of the film, the camera moves back, changing from close-up images to more distant ones. This is what you are trying to achieve through words.

The illustration below shows how this might work for *Legions of the Eagle*, shown as a director's storyboard. When you try out this kind of ending you could use the same technique.

1) Gaius, dressed in uniform, smiling.

2) Gaius leading his ten men and a little dog across a bridge over a broad river.

3) Long shot of the men walking away; a sunset on the horizon.

◆ Ending 3: *a possible sequel*

You can, of course, leave your story ending more open. This would allow you to write a SEQUEL to the story if you wanted to. This can be done easily, by ending your story with a question.

> *Paulina sighed. At least her problems with slaves appeared to be over now. Or were they?*
>
> *As Lucius thought back over the events of the last few days, he found it difficult to believe that some of these things had really happened. At that moment he sincerely believed that he'd seen the last of the mosaic maker. But had he?*

You can also create the same effect through dialogue between two characters. This time the story doesn't end with a question but with one character, usually the one who has the final word, making some comment that suggests the story could be continued at another time. Here's an example:

> *'Well, that's the end of that then,' Silvia remarked as they left the temple.*
> *'I wouldn't bet on it!' Livia replied with a laugh.*

◆ Ending 4: *the shock*

Another type of ending is the shock ending. This works by first making everything seem to be ordinary and as expected and then delivering something shocking and not at all what the reader was expecting. Here is an example:

> *Lytras left the arena. At last he was a free man. Life was good and the rest of the day stretched ahead of him, to do with as he pleased. Lytras stepped out into his new life and as he did so, failed to notice the cloaked figure which detached itself from the shadows of the tunnel and followed him. He didn't notice the dagger either. Until it was too late.*

◆ Ending 5: *and so ...*

The final technique for ending a story is for you to address your reader directly. This is the 'And so …' style of ending.

If you wrote your story using first person narrative, like Robert Graves' *I, Claudius*, then you could end your story with something like:

> *And so it was that I came to win my freedom.*

Or something like:

> *So, I finally understood why Marcia had been behaving so strangely. It had not been her fault and she had been trying to protect me all along. If only she had said something earlier, none of this would have happened.*

If you did not write your story in the first person, then it is the unseen narrator who closes the story. Here is an example:

> *And so it was that Lytras came to win his freedom. His story became well known throughout the Roman world, but even though it really happened, there are days when Lytras himself finds it all hard to believe.*

Or maybe:

> *So, Paulina finally understood why Marcia had behaved so very strangely. The poor girl had misunderstood what she had overheard and, in an attempt to protect her mistress, had felt compelled to replace the missing amber necklace by whatever means she could. If only she had confided her fears, none of this terrible business need ever have happened.*

ACTIVITY

1 Discuss with the rest of your class the strengths and weaknesses of each type of ending described on pages 36–39.
2 Choose two different techniques and use them to write two different endings to a story.
3 Which type do you think you'll use in your story? Why?

◆ *Practise using setting – in a mosaic workshop*

PETRONIUS

I'm glad you've had time to visit the mosaic workshop. We expect great things from our business. As you probably know, a mosaic floor is made up of hundreds of small coloured pieces of stone, TESSERAE, laid to make designs and pictures. These used to be made in just black and white but our workshop is starting to experiment with other colours.

There are two basic methods of laying a mosaic floor. One is to set the coloured *tesserae* in the wet mortar on the floor on site, a small area at a time. The other, which we use for detailed work, is to glue the *tesserae* face down onto a cloth. This can be done in the workshop, just as you see Marcus doing here. Marcus is working on the corner detail for a villa's dining room floor. It shows a male figure who represents winter.

When Marcus has finished, this mosaic will be taken by cart to the villa site. There, it will be laid on the wet mortar on the floor. Once the mortar has dried, the cloth will be peeled off, leaving the *tesserae* fixed in place. Then the *tesserae* will be ground and polished to produce the final finished surface, a beautiful mosaic floor that will last for centuries.

SOURCE I An artist's illustration of a mosaic workshop.

40

SOURCE II Types of rock or stone used to provide different coloured *tesserae*. Some of these would be available locally; others were brought in from elsewhere in Britain or the wider Roman Empire.

black/grey – hard lias

brown – soft shaley ironstone

red – tile, baked clay

yellow – baked chalk

white – limestone or chalk

SOURCE III A reconstruction of a mosaic workshop in the museum at Corinium (present-day Cirencester). As well as this workshop, there would be a yard for storage and a drawing office or library of designs plus a space for the clerks who handled orders and accounts.

ACTIVITY

1 Look at Source I. Some historical fiction is illustrated. If this was the illustration on the left-hand page of an historical novel, what would the narrative on the facing page say? Write it. The rest of the sources and information on these two pages will help you.

2 Look at Source III, the museum reconstruction.
   ◆ What tools are being used by the mosaic maker?
   ◆ What evidence might the museum curators have based this reconstruction upon?

◆ *Practise plot development – in the bakery*

SOURCE I The *PISTRINA* (bakery) of Modestus in Pompeii. This was one of 35 *pistrinas* in Pompeii.

Grain was put into the top of the egg-timer-shaped top stone, the CANTILAS, and this turned on the cone-shaped lower stone, the META. The ground flour was caught on the shelf below.

The flour was mixed with water, olive oil and yeast and formed into loaves which were baked in this oven. There were two grades of loaf, *PANIS CLIBANICUS* (high quality, made with white flour) and *PANIS PUERO* (made of left-overs). As well as plain bread, many bakers made loaves flavoured with seeds, nuts, herbs or spices.

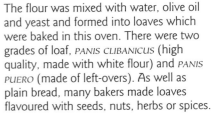

The MILL STONES were made from volcanic rock (grey-black tufa) and the *cantilas* was turned using wooden bars fitted into holes. This heavy work was done by donkeys or by slaves, usually convicts serving life sentences.

Many Roman houses were decorated with frescoes (wall paintings). Frescoes were painted using powdered PIGMENTS mixed with water. The resulting paint was applied to walls before the plaster had dried. When the plaster dried, the picture was fixed on the wall. Sources II and III are good examples.

SOURCE II Wall painting of a bakery in Pompeii giving out free bread, paid for by a wealthy citizen.

SOURCE III Wall painting of the baker Terentius Neo and his wife.

ACTIVITY

Look at Source II.
1 Think of this as a snapshot of an incident in your own story.
2 Think about what would happen after the bread has been given out. What might happen next?
3 In groups, decide on three possible developments in the plot.

◆ *Practise plot development – in the temple*

Our envoys need to travel to Rome to meet the Emperor Vespasian, but they have to know if tomorrow will be a safe day to set off. At today's ceremony, the *haruspex* will take the AUGURIES by sacrificing a goat and examining its entrails. If there is no sign of disease then it will be a good day to travel. As a priestess, I have to be at the ceremony. As you know, we Romans take our religion very seriously.

Now it is time to go. If you come home with me after the baths I will show you the LARARIUM, our household shrine to the spirit (*lar*) who protects us.

SILVIA

SOURCE I The ruins of a temple in Lectis Magna. Ceremonies such as that described by Silvia took place in the sacred space in front of the temple.

SOURCE II Roman gods and goddesses.

The Romans worshipped a number of gods and goddesses and believed that they influenced people's daily lives. Romans prayed, offered gifts and made sacrifices to their gods and goddesses, some of whom are listed here. They might also have consulted astrologers, rather like some people still do today.

Aesclepius	God of Medicine
Apollo	God of Music and the Sun
Bacchus	God of Wine
Ceres	Goddess of Corn and Harvests
Diana	Goddess of Hunting and the Moon
Jupiter	King of the Gods
Juno	Goddess of Women and Marriage
Mars	God of War
Mercury	God of Trade and Thieves
Minerva	Goddess of Wisdom
Neptune	God of the Sea
Pluto	God of Death
Venus	Goddess of Love and Beauty
Vesta	Goddess of the Hearth
Vulcan	God of Fire, Volcanoes and Metalworking

ACTIVITY

You are going to think of ideas for using Roman religious beliefs to develop the plot in your story.

◆ Perhaps one of your characters calls on a god for help.
◆ Perhaps an incident in your story takes place outside a temple or shrine.
◆ Perhaps your story takes place on a bad luck day, as in Mick Gower's *The Guard Dog Geese*.

You should write down at least one idea.

SOURCE III *A lararium.*

SOURCE IV A model of what the shrine built on Maiden Castle, just outside Durnovaria, may have looked like. (Model displayed in Dorset County Museum, Dorchester.)

Not all temples are grand buildings like Silvia's, of course. This is our local shrine in Durnovaria. Wherever you stand in the town you can see it up on the skyline.

PETRONIUS

45

◆ *Practise setting and dialogue – in the baths*

> I promised you some pampering and this is just the place for that, the public baths of Lectis Magna. Come on in with me. You might want to hire a slave to keep an eye on your clothes. There have been a lot of thefts recently.

SILVIA

SOURCE I   Sylvia's visit to the baths.

This is the women's baths. (It would be scandalous for men and women to bathe together.) Enter via a narrow corridor.

Change in *Apodyteria* (changing room)

Out to exercise in the PALAESTRA. Play a ball game. Eat pastry bought from the pastry seller.

Cleanse with oil and a STRIGIL. Massage.

Go into the TEPIDARIUM. Gossip with friends.

Quick plunge in the FRIGIDARIUM to close your pores.

SOURCE II An extract from the writings of Seneca (4BC–AD65) written *c.* AD50.

My lodgings are right over a public bath house. It's enough to make a man hate his own ears. First there are the strenuous types exercising, swinging lead weights about in their hands, and grunting and groaning.

Then there are the less athletic types having a massage. All you hear is the slap of the hands on shoulders, or some fellow who likes singing in the bath, or the oafs who dive into the pool with the highest leaps and biggest splashes.

ACTIVITY

Here is another chance to practise writing dialogue.
1 With a partner, devise a short conversation or describe an incident which takes place during Silvia's visit to the baths. You may remember that she found that wax tablet. Will you use that incident or another?
2 Be prepared to describe or narrate this to the rest of the class. You could even perform it like a play.

If you choose to include a visit to the baths in your story, remember that as a writer you are unlikely to describe the whole process because it would probably slow down the action. Your reader would feel that you were telling them some history and they would probably skip the description to get on with what happened next.

HOW TO WRITE

Off to the *LACONIUM* to work up a good sweat.

Sit and relax and sweat in the *CALDARIUM*.

Final dip in the swimming pool.

Get dressed and leave.

◆ *Practise settings and plot – in the theatre*

> *Salve!* Lytras here. I am in the theatre to save a seat for my master. He will be cool here in the shade of the awning and I have brought his cushion so he will be comfortable.
> I don't know what play is being performed this afternoon and obviously I will not be staying to watch. This afternoon I return to the gladiators' barracks for training.

SOURCE I The theatre in Curium. The artist has reconstructed part of the theatre to show what it would have looked like in Roman times. It had seats for approximately 3,500 people.

ⒶCTIVITY

Study Sources I to VI carefully.

1 Now put yourself in the sandals of Lytras' master going to the theatre in Curium to watch a performance of *The Slip-Knot* (see Source II).

2 Draw a cartoon strip to show your visit. You could use the cartoon strip showing Sylvia's visit to the baths in Lectis Magna on pages 46–47 as a model to help you. Make sure you put Sceparnio and Ampelisca in the correct colours. Where do you think the seats for the common people would be?

SOURCE II An extract from *The Slip-Knot*, a romantic comedy by the popular Roman playwright Plautus (254–184BC), written *circa* 193BC. He is said to have written more than 130 plays, of which 21 survive. His work inspired later playwrights such as William Shakespeare.

ACT II: SCENE IV

At the noise of the young girl Ampelisca's knocking, the elderly slave Sceparnio at last opens the door of his master's house.

SCEPARNIO: Who is the saucy knave that knocks like this?
AMPELISCA (with a curtsey): 'Tis I.
SCEPARNIO: Aha! A very dainty miss!
AMPELISCA: Good day, young cock!
SCEPARNIO: Good day, my little hen.

AMPELISCA: I've –
SCEPARNIO (interrupting): Come tonight. You will be welcome then.
Girls in the morning don't with me agree.
What do you say to that, my little chick-a-dee?
AMPELISCA: I say that you have too familiar grown.
SCEPARNIO: Good lord! It might be Venus' self come down.
O what a merry eye, and what a skin!
A bruinette – brunette, of course I mean.
How firm her breasts! Her mouth, how sweet it pouts!
AMPELISCA: Hands off! I am not meat for country louts.

SOURCE III   Bone theatre tickets. Plays were usually paid for by rich people; the common people got in free but had to sit in the poorer seats.

SOURCE IV   A mosaic from Pompeii showing actors preparing for a play. Opinions vary: some sources say that only men were actors, while others suggest that women acted on stage too.

SOURCE VI   In large theatres the actors' faces could not be seen clearly, so they wore masks with strong expressions to show what sort of character they were, male or female, happy or sad, and so on. Their costumes were coded: red robes for a poor person, purple robes for a rich person, plain tunics for slaves and several colours for a young person.

SOURCE V   An extract from *Last Act in Palmyra* by Lindsey Davis (1995). Marcus Didius Falco, the narrator, describes the orchestra.

Our orchestra consisted of Afrania the flautist, whose instrument was the single piped tibia; another girl who played panpipes; a gnarled, hook-nosed old chap whom I had seen clashing a pair of small hand-cymbals with an incongruous delicacy; and a pale young man who plucked the lyre when he felt like it. They were led by a tall, thin, balding character who sometimes boomed away on a big double wind instrument that had one pipe turned up at the end, whilst he beat time for the others with a foot clacker. This was a large group, compared with some theatre company ensembles, but allowed for the fact that the participants also danced, sold trays of limp sweetmeats, and offered entertainment afterwards to members of the audience.

VALE! FAREWELL!

Canidius helps you pull everything together in a well-structured, readable story

VESPASIAN

"I hope you have enjoyed your visit to my empire. I've heard good things about your work from Canidius. He says your writing shows promise. I look forward to reading your stories about my people and their lives. Now Canidius has just got some final words of advice for you. You have the Emperor's thanks.

Before you go, perhaps you would like to accept a **second challenge**. As you now know, life in my empire is good for the ordinary people. My reign is a peaceful and prosperous one. Sadly, my astrologers tell me the same will not be said of the reigns of many of my successors. Many of them will not be effective emperors. In fact, under them the Roman Empire will eventually fall apart.

So my second challenge to you is to find out what makes an effective Roman Emperor and at the same time to find out why the Roman Empire falls apart.

For the moment, *VALE!*"

ACTIVITY

Are you ready for Vespasian's second challenge? Your teacher has all the information you need to look at what makes an effective Roman Emperor and why the Roman Empire fell apart. If you have access to a computer it can be a computer-led investigation. If not, then it will use books and worksheets.

"I'm sure you've been paying attention to my advice during the book, but just in case, here is a checklist. It will remind you of all the things you need to do when writing your story."

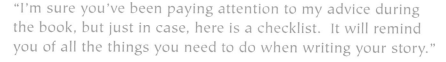

◆ *Story-writing checklist*

Characters:
* Not more than three.
* Think about personality and physical appearance.

Setting:
* Research the setting carefully.
* The action in the story might take place in more than one setting.
* Describe the settings carefully.

Problem:
This is what drives the narrative along, it starts off the plot.

* What is it that brings your characters together in your chosen setting?
* Make sure there really is a problem to solve. It needs to be believable and exciting. It could be a mystery to solve or a crisis of some kind to overcome.

Conflicts:
These are what happen because of the problem at the start of the story.

* Make sure that you use conflicts to make your plot interesting, and drive the story along.
* Use conflicts to develop your characters. How they behave will give your readers a sense of what they are like.
* Make sure that you don't have too many conflicts — three at the most.

Resolution:
* How does the problem finally get resolved?
* Is your ending believable and does it fit with the rest of your story?
* Think about the type of ending you use — will you leave the readers with a question, will there be a shock ending or will you gradually withdraw from the story, leaving the characters to get on with their own lives?

HOW TO WRITE

◆ Writer's notes

Make sure you have decided whether your story is going to be told in first person narrative by one of your characters, or by an unseen narrator using the third person.

Look at the story board and story plan that you constructed earlier. Will either of these form the skeleton of your Roman story?

SILVIA

PETRONIUS

PAULINA

LYTRAS

Characters

- ◆ Use the gingerbread technique to help you create your characters (see page 15).
- ◆ Read your description of a gladiator. Can you use him in your story?
- ◆ We have used some characters to guide you through Roman towns on pages 4–5. Do you want to use one of them?
- ◆ Look back at the dialogue you wrote (pages 24–29). Remember how it showed readers what the characters were like. Use this technique when you write dialogue for your characters in the Roman story.
- ◆ Use descriptive verbs and adverbs when you write about characters.
- ◆ Remember that similes can be an excellent way of suggesting what a character is like.

Setting

- ◆ Read your descriptions of a Roman market and street on pages 9 and 11. Can you use these in your story?
- ◆ Don't forget to use the illustrations in this book to help you create descriptions of setting. You can refer to artefacts used by the Romans to help you create a sense of place in your story.
- ◆ Remember that alliteration can be useful when describing places.
- ◆ Adjectives are excellent for creating strong descriptions of places, but be careful – don't use long lists of adjectives, they can get boring.

Problem

◆ What event or situation starts the story off and provides the reason for what the characters do?
◆ Look at some of the story problems described on page 19. Could you use one of these to help you plan your story?
◆ Is the problem about something that is lost?
◆ Could the problem be caused by something someone does?
◆ Is the problem a mystery to be solved?
◆ Is the problem a result of the characters' reactions to a natural disaster, accident or event?

Opening

When you have decided on your characters, setting and problem, make sure you think about how you will write your opening paragraph. Will you use:

◆ an *in medias res* opening
◆ dialogue
◆ an opening which sets the scene, like the opening shots of a film?

Look back at the work you did on story openings on pages 24–27. Can you use what you have written?

Conflicts

◆ What important things happen as a result of the initial problem?
◆ Are the things that happen believable and do they match your Roman setting?
◆ How do your characters cope with the conflicts?
◆ Look at the narratives you wrote to go with the illustrations on pages 41 or 43. Can you use these in your story?
◆ Look at the scene you wrote based on the game of Knucklebones on page 29. How did you develop that situation for the characters? Can you use the scene in your story?

Resolutions

◆ Has the problem been sorted out?
◆ Has everything important been explained?
◆ Think about your final paragraph. What sort of ending have you chosen? Will you leave things open for a sequel, provide a shock or move the reader gently away from your characters, like the closing shots of a film?
◆ Look at the endings you wrote on page 39. Could any of these be used in your story?

◆ *What have you learned about the history of the Roman Empire?*

Not only have you written a piece of historical fiction but you've also learnt a lot about towns, work, trade, entertainment and people in the Roman Empire. You are now going to think about what you have found out.

Petronius, tell my assistants what life is like for you in the Roman Empire.

How **comfortable** are you?

I live in a comfortable house and because I am quite well off I have enough to eat and drink and good warm clothing. When the *aqueduct* is completed, I will have clean water to drink.

Do you have to **work** hard?

I do not have to work as hard as when I was in the army. Now I just need to supervise the slaves on my farm and in my house and, of course, keep a check on the mosaic workshop.

What do you do for **enjoyment**?

For entertainment, there are my friends in the tavern and at the baths plus the games in the *amphitheatre*, although those do not take place very often.

What **dangers and suffering** do you face?

There is always the danger of disease. Here in Britain we did not get too involved in the civil wars but there is always the possibility of a revolt like that by Boudicca and of raids by barbarians from outside the empire.

How **free** are you?
Are you **equal** to other people?

As an ex-legionary, I am a full Roman citizen entitled to vote in local elections. This makes me superior to non-citizens and slaves.

ACTIVITY A

The questions above show you five headings which you could use for looking at life in the Roman Empire.

1 Work in groups to think of aspects of life in the Roman Empire which belong under each heading. For example:

◆ **comfort** – think about things that made life hard for some people or which made life comfortable for others

◆ **work** – think about different kinds of jobs that people did and whether they were good jobs (– you could say whether you think people worked hard or not)

◆ **enjoyment** – think about how ordinary people enjoyed themselves

◆ **danger** – think about the dangers people faced

◆ **freedom and equality** – think about whether people were free and whether Roman society was a place of equality or inequality.

2 Draw up lists under each heading. Your teacher can give you a set of statements to get you started. You could also get some ideas from what Petronius has to say (see above).

3 For each of these headings, think about how Roman life in AD78 compares with present-day life in your country.

4 Life in the Roman Empire was different for different people. Think about what your main character might have said about each of these topics. Would they have said the same as Petronius?

◆ *The History Writer's Skills*

ACTIVITY B

The activities in this book have been designed to improve your history writing skills.

1 Look carefully at the History Writer's Skills Wall below.

◆ Which new skills have you learned through studying this book?
◆ Which skills have you improved?
◆ Which skills do you need to develop further?

2 Do you have enough skills to reconstruct Roman history? Before you begin your next history topic, design an action plan for yourself. Set yourself three targets to improve your work in history and list the skills that you will need to practise to reach these targets.

I can explain why an event happened by discussing several reasons.

I organise my research effectively. I know which questions to ask to check the reliability of sources.

I know how to structure narrative.

I support my argument with evidence.

I can use ICT tools to amend and refine my work.

I can find out about the past from a range of sources, including the Internet and CD-ROMs.

I know how to use strong and descriptive verbs to improve my writing.

I can identify changes over time.

I can write in the first person.

I can identify some of the different ways in which the past is represented.

I know what makes a good story.

I can write descriptions of places in the past.

I can describe some of the characteristic features of people in the past.

I can write a third person narrative.

◆ *Glossary*

ADJECTIVE   a word or phrase which describes or modifies a noun

ADVERB   a word or phrase which describes or modifies a verb

ALLITERATION   a phrase where adjacent or closely related words begin with the same phoneme (letter sound)

AMPHITHEATRE   a building, usually circular, with tiers of seats rising from a central open space

APODYTERIA   changing rooms in the Roman baths

AQUEDUCT   channel to carry water

ARCHAEOLOGIST   someone who studies people from the past by looking at the sites where they lived and the physical remains of their society

AUGURIES   omens or signs believed to predict future events

BASILICA   town hall

CADUCEUS   red-hot iron

CALDARIUM   hot bath

CANTILAS   top stone of flour mill

CENA   dinner, the main meal of the day

CHARLATAN   someone who pretends to be an expert

CIRCA or C.   round about, used today by historians to show that they do not know the precise date of an event – circa 193BC means round about that date

COBNUTS   hazel nuts

CONJUNCTION   a word used to link sentences or clauses or to connect words within the same phrase

DIALOGUE   conversation

ENTRAILS   internal organs of an animal

FORUM public place, often used as a marketplace and centre of public business

FREEDMAN former slave who has been freed

FRIGIDARIUM cold bath

FULLER'S EARTH a special kind of clay used for cleaning cloth

GALLEY Roman ship powered by oars as well as sail

GUSTATIO starter course of dinner

HARUSPEX a priest who examines the entrails of animal sacrifices for omens from the gods

HORAE the twelve equal sections a Roman day was divided into

IENTCULUM breakfast

IN MEDIAS RES in the middle of things – the writer takes the reader straight into the action of a story

LACONIUM hot steam room

LARARIUM shrine housing the spirit (*lar*) who protects the household

MENSA PRIMA main course of dinner

MENSA SECUNDA dessert course of dinner

META bottom, cone-shaped stone of flour mill

MILL STONES stones used to grind wheat to make flour

MOSAIC a design, in Roman times a floor, made up of hundreds of small coloured pieces of stone, laid to make designs and pictures

MULSUM entrée

NARRATIVE a re-telling of events

PALAESTRA exercise yard

PANIS CLIBANICUS good quality loaf of bread

PANIS PUERO poor quality loaf of bread

PESTLE tool for grinding food

PIGMENT paint, colouring matter

PISTRINA bakery

PORTICO — a porch in front of the entrance to a building

PRANDIUM — lunch

PULMENTUM — a vegetable stew made from peas, beans and lentils

REPORTING CLAUSE — phrase that indicates reported speech, such as 'he said', 'she shouted'

SALVE — hello

SALVETE — hello when speaking to more than one person

SCRIBE — writer or clerk

SEQUEL — a continuation of a story, play, film, etc.

SIMILE — comparison of one thing with another, usually involving 'as' or 'like'

STRIGIL — curved blade used to scrape the body after bathing

TALI — dice for playing knucklebones

TEPIDARIUM — warm room in baths

TESSERAE — small coloured pieces of stone used to make up a mosaic

THERMOPOLIUM — snack bar

THESAURUS — a book containing lists of words with the same or similar meanings

TOGA — piece of cloth draped around the body

TRIDENT — three-pronged spear

VALE — goodbye

VALETE — goodbye when speaking to more than one person

VERB — word or group of words that names an action or state of being

VILLA — a Roman farm and the house associated with it

◆ Index

THIS IS HISTORY!

◆ Titles in the series:

◆ Acknowledgements

The Publishers would like to thank the following for permission to reproduce copyright material:

Pictures:
p.10 *all* Dave Martin; p.11 Museum of London; p.14 The Moviestore Collection; p.16 *t* R Sheridan/Ancient Art and Architecture Collection Ltd, *b* R Sheridan/Ancient Art and Architecture Collection Ltd; p.18 The Watts Publishing Group; p.26 Dave Martin; p.28 *t* R Sheridan/Ancient Art and Architecture Collection Ltd, *b* C M Dixon; p.30 Dave Martin; p.32 Penguin Books Ltd; p.33 *t* C M Dixon, *b* C M Dixon; p.41 Corinium Museum, Cirencester; p.42 *tl* Dave Martin, *tr* Dave Martin, *b* C M Dixon; p.43 *t* C M Dixon, *b* C M Dixon; p.44 R Sheridan/Ancient Art and Architecture Collection Ltd; p.45 *t* Scala Group, *b* The Dorset County Museum; p.48 C M Dixon; p.49 *t* Werner Forman Archive, J Paul Getty Museum, Malibu, USA, *l* R Sheridan/Ancient Art and Architecture Collection Ltd, *b* C M Dixon; p.57 Dave Martin

(*t* = top, *b* = bottom, *l* = left, *r* = right, *c* = centre)

Written sources:
p.7 *Source I* Marilyn Todd, *Man Eater*, Pan, 1997, *Source II* Extract from *Two for the Lions* by Lindsey Davis, published by Arrow/Hutchinson. Used by permission of The Random House Group Limited; p.10 *Source IV* Extract from *Venus in Copper* by Lindsey Davis, published by Arrow/Hutchinson. Used by permission of The Random House Group Limited; p.12 *Source I* Extract from *Venus in Copper* by Lindsey Davis, published by Arrow/Hutchinson. Used by permission of The Random House Group Limited;

p.13 *Source II* Rosemary Sutcliff, *The Mark of the Horse Lord*, Puffin, in association with Oxford University Press, 1965; p.14 *Source III* Steven Saylor, *A Murder on the Appian Way*, Constable and Robinson Publishing Ltd, *Source V* Extract from *Two for the Lions* by Lindsey Davis, published by Arrow/Hutchinson. Used by permission of The Random House Group Limited; p.24 Extract from *Last Act in Palmyra* by Lindsey Davis, published by Arrow/Hutchinson. Used by permission of The Random House Group Limited; p.26 *Source II* Extract from *The Silver Pigs* by Lindsey Davis, published by Arrow/Hutchinson. Used by permission of The Random House Group Limited; p.30 *Source I* Extract from *Poseidon's Gold* by Lindsey Davis, published by Arrow/Hutchinson. Used by permission of The Random House Group Limited; p.31 *Source III* Extract from *The Capricorn Bracelet* by Rosemary Sutcliff, published by Red Fox. Used by permission of The Random House Group Limited; p.32 Robert Graves, *I Claudius*, AP Watt Ltd; p.36 Extract from *Sparks: The Guard Dog Geese* by Mick Gowar, first published in the UK by Franklin Watts in 1997, a division of the Watts Publishing Group Limited, 96 Leonard Street, London, EC2A 4XD; p.37 Henry Treece, *Legions of the Eagle*, Penguin, 1965, by permission of John Johnson Limited; p.48 *Source II* Plautus, *The Slip-Knot*, Routledge, 1925; p.49 *Source V* Extract from *Last Act in Palmyra* by Lindsey Davis, published by Arrow/Hutchinson. Used by permission of The Random House Group Limited.